Books by Gary Beck

Novels

Acts of Defiance
Extreme Change
Flawed Connections
Call to Valor
Sudden Conflicts
Crumbling Ramparts
Flare Up
Raise High the Walls
Still Defiant
State of Rage
Wave Length
Protective Agency
Obsess
Still Obsessed
Rescue Me
Until the Bell
Rescue Others
Pirate Spring

Poetry Collections

Expectations
Days of Destruction
Dawn in Cities
Assault on Nature
Songs of a Clerk
Civilized Ways
Conditioned Response
Displays
Perceptions
Fault Lines
Tremors
Unillumined
Perturbations
Blossoms of Decay
Rude Awakenings
Blunt Force
Remission of Order
Contusions
Transitions
Earth Links
Mortal Coil
Desperate Seeker
Too Harsh For Pastels
Temporal Dreams
Severance
Redemption Value
Fractional Disorder
Disruptions
Ignition Point
Learning Curve
Resonance
Turbulence
Lacerations
State of the Union
Purpose
Double Envelopment
Unveilings
Discoveries
Virtual Living
Molecular Distortion
Glimpses
Objectives
Rigors

Rigors

Gary Beck

ISBN: 978-93-6354-620-2

First Edition: 2025
Rs. 200/-

Cyberwit.net
HIG 45 Kaushambi Kunj, Kalindipuram
Allahabad - 211011 (U.P.) India
http://www.cyberwit.net
Tel: +(91) 9415091004
E-mail: info@cyberwit.net

Printed at Repro India Limited.

To all the true poets who try to fit into

The maddening world

Poems from Rigors have appeared in

Bewildering Stories, Dissident Voice, Highland Park Poetry (Muses Gallery), Mad Swirl, Polseguera Magazine, Setu Magazine, The Seventh Quarry Poetry Magazine, The Soliloquist Journal, Verbal Art (Authors Press), Winamop Magazine, Zin Daily (Zvonay Nari Cultural Production Coop

Play Collections

The Big Match and other one act plays
Collected Plays of Gary Beck Volume I
Collected Plays of Gary Beck Volume II
Collected Plays of Gary Beck Volume III

Translations

Four Plays by Jean Baptiste Moliere (Directed by Gary Beck)
Three Plays by Aristophanes (Directed by Gary Beck)
Sophocles-Three Plays (Directed by Gary Beck)
Agamemnon: The Play by Aeschylus (Directed by Gary Beck)

Short Story Collections

A Glimpse of Youth and other stories
Now I Accuse and other stories
Dogs Don't Send Flowers and other stories
Judgments and other stories

Essays

The Republic of Dreams and other essays
Collected Essays

Poetry Chapbooks

Remembrance and other Poems
The Conquest of Somalia
The Dance of Hate and Other Poems

Contents

Disorder

Gunshots echo again
as we huddle on the floor
hoping the street battle
will be over soon
before bullets penetrate
the walls of our apartment
in public housing.
Almost every night now
shooting starts after dark
so we don't dare go outside
at risk of getting shot,
except for emergencies.
If my children get sick
and need a doctor,
no matter how dangerous
the trip to the hospital
I have to do it for them
because ambulances
don't come here anymore.

Resources

The big storm finally came
and blew out the power.
The streets are impassable.
I'm stuck in my apartment
without electricity
so I can't charge my phone,
my laptop, my kindle.
I don't know anyone
in this building of strangers,
so I can't visit someone
to pass the time away.
I'm going out of my mind
because there's nothing to do
and I can't help worrying
what will happen to me
if the power doesn't come back.

Beauty

I see the tarnished city
streets overflowing
with legions of the lost,
homeless veterans
yearning for their uniforms,
illegal immigrants
hope ignited at the Rio Grande,
extinguished at the detention center,
the mentally ill, the criminals,
the endless victims of poverty
circumspectly ignored
by citizens of abundance
subtracted from humanity,
guilty of the primal sin
abandonment of the children.
All these horrors parade
before my scavenged eyes,
then I turn a corner,
walk past a neglected park,
halted by a flash of orange
a Monarch butterfly,
a visitor of beauty,
a feast for my famished soul,
a momentary fantasy
of pollinating away
the pestilential ugliness
that pollutes the urb.

Apprehension

Summer is almost over
and the departing juices
that invigorate me
now warn me to prepare
for the long, cold winter
that will chill my bones
which so ravage my body
I'm not sure I'll survive
to taste another spring.

Choices

I lived with my husband
for six pain-filled years
of constant abuse,
verbal and physical,
until I divorced him.
Then he started death threats.
First were unsigned letters,
words cut from magazines
promising torture.
Next were obscene phone calls
vowing he would kill me.
I went to the police,
talked to a detective,
showed him all the letters,
described all the phone calls,
but all he could suggest,
an order of protection
that he said wouldn't do much good,
which left me only one choice
to get a pistol
and learn to use it.

Housing Crisis

The inexorable plan
of the corporate magnates
to gentrify the cities
continues relentlessly,
lower income residents
forced out of their apartments
by inordinate rent hikes,
until all they can afford
are outer borough buildings
far removed from former jobs,
so travel is too costly
for them to go to work,
leaving urban centers
as the playground for the rich,
labor imported daily,
not allowed to live there.

Job Bound

I work remotely
five days a week,
with overtime
when I can't finish
my daily quota.
I keep getting phone calls
that I have to answer
for important problems
that I didn't used to get
when I worked at the office
before Covid.
Too many distractions
interrupt the work day
and affect the performance
of my regular duties
to serve our clients.
I worry that my boss
won't be happy
at interrupted tasks
because I need this job
to pay my bills,
so I'll do my best
despite disruptions
to my employer's time.

Product Placement

Many people buy art
for investment
and go through the pretense
of loving art
to fool their friends,
some of whom buy
for a different reason,
to show off their taste
hanging on their walls.
When art is an item
to only be acquired
by how much you can spend
it just resembles
commodities,
except proud owners
won't display
pork bellies
for guest's enjoyment.

Lessons

When I was a young man
unlike many people
I tasted luxury,
although most of my life
I lived in poverty.

I was fortunate to learn
before I pursued wealth
I did not need Picassos,
I did not need Warhols.
If the need arose
to look at art
I'd go to a museum.

When the rich purchase art
to aggrandize their lives,
they hang it on their walls,
but after a few days
they no longer notice
expensive acquisitions.

No matter how much we amass
some of us realize
possessions are ephemeral
and those who delude themselves
with accumulation of things
must leave everything behind
just like everyone else.

Resigned

Everything was simple
when I was younger.
I still liked cold weather
and just put on a sweater
unless it was freezing.
Now it takes longer
to get dressed to go out
and I don't like the cold,
even when it's not that cold.
I must accept how it is
no matter how unpleasant
reality has become
because there is no choice,
denial would breed bitterness
poisoning remaining days.

Alarm Bells

The safety of the world
is daily more dangerous,
North Korean missiles
flying over Japan,
the President of Russia
threatens nuclear weapons
to subdue the Ukraine,
extreme terrorist groups
export death and destruction
to the people of the West
especially America,
a blundering giant
growing emaciated
by raucous divisions
themed by lies and hatred
that dilute abilities
to solve our problems,
while lurking in the East
China watches our discord
and plans to replace us,
with our cooperation.

Greed

The glaciers are melting.
The seas are rising.
Storms get bigger,
far more destructive.
Wild fires get wilder,
drought across the land,
natural disasters
increasing daily,
but the powers that be
will cease to profit
if we take urgent steps
to avert climate change,
preferring the collapse
of our environment,
rather than give up
exercising power,
wallowing in comforts.

Economic Threat

American railroads
once the only sure way
to cross the country,
have been mostly replaced
by impatient passengers
with airline travel.
But railroad owners
are making record profits
hauling vital freight
that keeps the nation going,
yet they will not fairly share
the money that enriches them
with railroad employees
who get almost no sick time
while giving their best
to demanding jobs.
Though most unions in our land
have lost power to the bosses
if the railroad workers strike
they will paralyze the nation
still struggling with inflation,
as well as other burdens
in a time of division.

Last Stop

When I was young
I could not foresee
how I'd end my days,
barely conscious
in a hospital bed,
in a nursing home
for the indigent,
staffed by the indifferent
of minimal service
to the ebbing lives
consigned to their care.
I can still cognate
sometimes when I'm clear,
but looking backwards
cannot determine
what I should have done
for a better ending.

Polluted Minds

It's midterm Election Day
and unlike years ago
when people did not know
who they would vote for
until the last minute
when they reached the polls
today we are certain,
the country so polarized
most of us are decided
not always for good reasons,
some full of anger and hate
spewing ugly theories
of evil conspiracies
plotting to enslave them,
encouraged by a few
who want to end democracy,
replace it with autocracy,
so they can tell us what to do
then compel us to obey
either with illegal laws,
or unjustified arrests,
urgent to shatter the idea
of a free society.

Systemic Failures

Winter will be coming soon.
We lack fuel for power, heat
and our leaders are away
on luxurious vacations,
or going through the motions
of pretending to govern.
We don't know how to get help
as our suffering gets worse.
When freezing weather arrives
many of us will perish,
especially the aging,
while righteous politicians
continue their promises
of aid in our time of need.

United We...

The pressure on Americans
continues to accelerate
undermining security
until we are so distracted
from the problems of the future
that we neglect the procedures
to ensure a safe tomorrow.
So many threats that affect us:
Covid, hurricanes, Monkey Pox,
wild fires, resurging polio.
The chaos of our politics
prevents agreement, compromise,
leaving voters in confusion
about the real issues we face,
instead demanding we take sides
with one of the disputing groups
rather than cooperating
to achieve vital solutions
to the impending disasters
that will devastate our nation
if we do not join together
and end the dangerous impasse
that will destroy the promised dream.

Helpers

I lie on confine bed
and ring for the nurse
who does not answer.
I am cold, shivering,
wet from my waste,
feeling awful.
I wait and wait
but no one comes.
This has happened before
in a place of lost hope
and I must accept
whatever happens,
for no one will help me
in my time of decline.

Labor Relations

The company fired me
for trying to unionize
unprotected workers.
Many of them told me
they'd like to join
but they didn't want
to lose their jobs.
I tried to convince them
their only security
from corporate abuse
was to stand together
and support each other,
but they knew the company
opposed unionization
and were afraid if they joined
there'd be retaliation.
When the company fired me
no one else took my place
to sign up union members,
so the corporation won
because workers wouldn't resist
and now will only get
whatever scraps they're given.

Misleading

The invention of gunpowder
for use on the battlefield
changed the nature of war
which became more destructive,
since a hail of bullets
was far more destructive
than a hail of arrows
and death by friendly fire
of soldiers and commanders,
occurred more frequently
with the new technology,
but didn't answer the question:
How can gunfire be friendly?
If a bullet hits someone
I don't think they really care
whether it's from friend or foe.
Their loved ones don't feel better
when they find out painfully
their husband, brother, son
was killed by a buddy.
We should drop the word 'friendly'
that doesn't make death easier,
place the blame where it should be,
take responsibility
for wrongful fatality
and call it 'same side' fire,
so at least we'll know
where the shots came from
that weren't friendly.

Winged Pleasures

No matter what's wrong
with me, my land, the world
it's briefly forgotten
on a wonderful park day
sighting beautiful birds
(the avian kind,
  not nubile lasses).
I don't make judgments
like which one is best,
but I tend to be partial
towards non-migrators,
cardinals, jays, woodpeckers,
yet can't help enjoying
juncos, the tufted titmouse,
other transitories,
specially chickadees,
one of my favorite birds.
Most don't like to be looked at
so it's a great treat
to see and hear them,
enriching my day.

Standards

I never had a good teacher
when I was in grade school
and only one in high school,
who they fired right away
when he dared to deviate
from the curriculum
by discussing social issues
related to the books we read.
Now I sincerely hope
that many other students
had really good teachers,
if so they should be well paid,
of course never as much
as professional athletes,
since it's much more important
to hit a ball, throw a pass,
than to teach math or science.
But there is a difference.
Sports people must produce
or they are soon dismissed.
That fact doesn't apply
to schoolteachers anywhere
who hang on forever
blighting students lives,
almost never fired.
Perhaps we should give big bucks
to inspiring teachers,
measuring their success

by student's accomplishments,
fire the non-productive
and hire new-comers
eager to teach the young.

Efforts

We can't go back and right the wrongs
once inflicted on others.
What was done in ignorance
can never be rectified
no matter how much we regret
the harm we know we have done.
All we can attempt to do
is try to become better
and continue to do our best
to improve life for everyone
as we atone for misdeeds past.

Who Will Guard

A sane society
wouldn't let police officers
stand around helplessly
while children were being shot
in a school invasion
by a violent madman.
We cannot feel secure
for the safety of children
when they are in school
if we are not confident
in the dangerous event
of a lunatic intruder
entering the school,
opening fire on students,
while the police do not go in
to protect the children
who can't defend themselves.

Victims

The hatred that pervades our land
festers like an infected wound,
angry red, ready to erupt
and corrupt our tainted system.
The people who infect us
with the disease of violence
do not care the harm we suffer.
When the collaborating tools
that pervert our democracy
are suddenly revealed to us
they always blame someone else
never the manipulators
who instigate our divisions,
no longer restrained by reason
in an emotional climate
that devours the security
of the American people
who only want a better life
promised by the Constitution,
whose efforts to labor for it
have been summarily betrayed
by the greedy Lords of Profit
who refused to tolerate
the accumulation of wealth
by the middle and working class
that interferes with the hunger
to accumulate more and more.

Dwindling

In summer I forget
how the change of seasons
affects me differently,
for now that I am old
I suffer from the cold,
my brittle bones ailing
from lower temperature,
my easily chilled body
wears many layers
when I go outdoors.
I cover my legs
with a comforter
when I sit on the couch.
I often day dream
of tropical climes
apprehensive of
the coming ice age.

Supply Side Economics

Prices keep going up
while income remains the same
making some of us question
the reasons for rising costs.
If it was just milk or gas
we understand price controls,
but it's more than commodities.
Americans should get
a better explanation
why we're paying so much
for meat, eggs, other items,
besides blaming inflation.
When the cost of gas goes up
we know it costs truckers more
to make their deliveries.
Yet why don't costs go down
when the price of gas goes down?
We suspect that producers
make the same when cost goes up
and the middle men make the most,
while proportionately
retailers make the same
leaving the consumers
who can afford it least
to pay the highest prices.

Abundance

American consumers
who can afford to shop
are more numerous
than in other countries
and indulge themselves
in acquiring goods
in enormous quantities
preparing for disasters
that may or may not come,
but no matter what happens
they will not do without
as long as they can pay.

Shock

The day that summer ended
suddenly became much colder
and everywhere I walked
throughout the chilling city
I heard the bird's distress
as the warmth quickly failed,
but loudest of all were the blue jays,
screeching to each other
'who turned off the heat?'

Subjugation

I never thought I saw it all,
just enough not to envy
what I didn't have, didn't get.
I learned the hard way not to want,
to resist the desire for things
that drives us to accumulate
goods and services that sate,
without bringing fulfillment.
I will try harder every day
to restrain my vast appetite
for the treasures tv offers
that I am conditioned to want
until I am enslaved by greed
for what I really do not need.

Nursing Home

The faces are bleak.
Their last song
played long ago.
They lie in prison bed
reluctantly awaiting
to be collected
by the death service,
the final resolution
of incapacity.

Disillusion

Another election year
midterm, but still important
for the major parties
battling for control
of the Senate and House.
They attack each other
in virulent tv ads
that confuse the people
who no longer understand
how their government works,
while too many suspect
it no longer works for them.

Market Price

In the Information Age
everyone watches tv,
are constantly bombarded
to buy some kind of product.
Video presentations
slick, sleek, very watchable,
so cleverly constructed
we treat as entertainment,
many of us unaware
we are manipulated
to buy what they're showing us
whether we need their item,
or they're even good for us.

Respite

A beautiful fall day
in a troubled city
beleaguered by
constant threats of Covid
keeping some people masked,
inflation of food prices
making many struggle
to provide healthy meals,
crime proliferating
poverty populations
driven to desperation
resorting to violence
in the search for cash,
murder, rape, assault
all adding to tensions,
yet people are smiling today
some even saying hello,
a pleasant interval
in the urban climate.

Credo

Once again
at the doctor's office.
Resentful eyes follow me
because I was called first.
I don't know the other patients
so I don't care how they feel.
My illness is more than enough
to make me struggle every day
to keep up my good spirits
no matter how bad I feel
and never give in
to adversity.

Outreach

No matter how hard we try
to get along with others
it depends on acceptance
of differences between us.
If we could be tolerant
of someone else's views
distasteful to our beliefs
we might find accommodation,
despite urges of refusal.
It is useful to remember
that the wars of religion
that wracked the West
for hundreds of years
have mostly subsided
and have been replaced
by political strife
not as fanatic,
almost as stubborn.

There's No Place...

The Secret Police in Russia
conscript citizens on the streets
and send them to the army
to fight in the Ukraine.
The Morality Police
patrol the streets in Iran
and arrest citizens
who violate sharia.
Throughout the conflicted world
oppressive governments
persecute their citizens
who want a little freedom.
In the divided U.S.A.
some of us have forgotten
the values that protect us
from illegal seizure.

Fading

Summer is over.
Rays of warmth are departing,
not to return for many months.
The days and nights get colder
until chill courses my bones
that refuse to carry me.
I sit in torn armchair
in tattered overcoat,
wrapped in blankets
and do not know
if I will see the spring.

Neglect

The pandemic is over
they keep telling us,
but 400 people a day
are dying of Covid
and health authorities
leave it up to the public
to take preventive measures.
If elected officials
and the 1%
were part of the 400
we'd have an emergency
with all kinds of laws,
all kind of resolutions
to protect the privileged
from catching the disease.

The Prevalence of Greed

Election day is over.
The winners are happy
getting another term
or a new position.
The cries of: 'I've been robbed,
the election was stolen',
haven't hit the airwaves yet.
If we didn't know better
we would appreciate
democracy in action,
but some of the losers,
election deniers,
are preparing to protest
the elections they lost,
a painful reminder
individual greed
is far more important
than the needs of the nation.

Sore Losers

Election candidates
for governor and senate
refuse to declare
they'll abide by results
of the coming election,
setting a precedent
for any competition,
whether for the presidency,
sports events like football,
or children's classroom tests,
for the loser to assert:
'I didn't lose. It was stolen',
giving some a second chance
to reject reality.

Too Much

Daily disasters
assault the public
until we can't digest
the ongoing events,
fire, floods, crime, violence,
that overwhelm our systems
so we don't respond
to urgent demands
that require action
to preserve our country,
struggling to survive
political divisions,
diminishing resources,
increasing poverty,
threats to democracy
endangering the future
of our once proud nation.

Inflation

I was notified
in my email
that Social Security
went up 1½ %.
When I went to the store
milk, butter, cheese, eggs, bread
had gone up 35 %,
so I couldn't get everything
that we needed.
Rent went up 16%,
yet it has to be paid.
Better to be hungry
than to be put on the street.
Economists on tv
tell us prices will go down,
but landlords don't listen.
I know I'm not alone
in this difficult time,
but something should be done
to feed our families.

Interlude

A walk in the park.
The air is cleaner
than gasolined streets.
The leaves have not fallen
so from concealment
Cardinals call each other.
Robins on the ground
hunt for succulent worms.
Blue Jays squawk triumphantly
having stolen something.
It is a peaceful day.
People are smiling,
the fear of Covid forgotten,
a refreshing change
from the grim reality
of life in the city.

Shock II

On the visit to grandma
I walk through the nursing home
and hear moans of despair
behind some of the closed doors.
The elderly infirm
lie in containing beds
barely able to move,
spastic twitches
the only reminder
that life still remains,
however precarious.
I understand
pre-death hulkers
awaiting release
could not be helped at home,
but can't help wondering
if there is a better way
to store the outworn.

Public Well Being

The right to peaceful protest
should always be guaranteed
in a democracy,
which helps keep people free.
The outbreak of riots
should never be allowed
in a sane society,
since it usually leads
to violent disorders,
looting and arson.

When the disturbed assemble
then directly assault
the fabric of a nation,
losing control, running wild,
destroying property,
they terrify citizens
who rely on the state
to protect them from harm.

The hysterical demands
to defund the police
is a dangerous attack
on public safety,
a fragile condition
entirely dependent
on good government.

The nature of some men
perverted by ignorance,
motivated by anger
viciously directed
at peaceful citizens,
who must be protected
from depredation
that disrupt stability.

The groups of the lawless
who run wild in our streets
are seeking to destroy
our imperfect system
that despite many failings
frequently does its best
to nurture all of us,
guarded by the police
from those who want disorder
to end our way of life.

Planning

No matter how hard I try
I can't get a better job.
Either no experience,
I'm over qualified,
or most often, not hiring.
I took out a student loan
to pay for my education,
the road to a better life,
at least that's what they told me
when they suggested college
instead of joining the Army.
Now I'm no kind of scholar,
busted my ass in high school
in order to graduate,
then worked hard for my degree
which I got by working hard.
Either I fooled myself,
or the system fooled me
that a liberal arts grad
would easily find a good job.
At present in my life
it doesn't do me much good
to blame myself, or others.
I've got to figure out
how to change what's happening,
or spend the rest of my life
working for minimum wage.

Beast Plaint

We finally got one
after months of waiting,
unit 2300HD,
the household robot.
We had a Roomba
for a long time
and we used to laugh
when it chased the cat
and Mr. Ruffles
jumped on the sofa
to escape the monster.
The manufacturer claims
that the robot won't harm pets.
We'll have to wait and see.
But it's going to be funny
watching the robot
chase Mr. Ruffles.

Forced Quietude

In prosperous neighborhoods
the well-to-do leave the city
for holiday weekends,
the long, hot summer,
leaving empty streets,
stores shut lacking customers.
The few remaining people
talk overly loud
in times of abandonment.

Collision

Another car accident
in the Covid stressed city.
The uninjured drivers
angrily blamed each other,
cursing and accusing
of a deliberate crash,
immediately followed
by furious denials
and they started fighting.
One man was badly beaten.
He ran to his car,
took out a pistol,
began firing wildly,
hit a woman watching,
quickly ran away
from one more incident
that became violent
because we no longer know
when it's an accident
it's not done on purpose.

Lost Ideal

Winning or losing
is the end result
of competition
and at every level
if there is integrity
the outcome should be accepted
because tradition holds
it shouldn't be about
victory or defeat,
but how the game is played.

Fragile System

American Democracy
is not guaranteed
to continue indefinitely,
despite the constitution
and the promise
of that great document
that relies on the good will
of the owners of our land
to share with our people,
ruthlessly manipulated
by the lords of profit
who want their candidates
to be elected
and preserve the illusion
we are free people
who will fare better
with the rule of autocrats
who dismiss the contract,
majority rule,
minority rights.

Betrayal

Election Day comes soon,
yet the candidates
are ominously silent
about corporate earnings
that are exceedingly high
in a time of inflation.
We the people suffer
paying more and more at the store
until we can't afford
to feed our families
nourishing, healthy food,
while record profits
enrich executives,
as the rest of us
are betrayed again
by the greedy servants
of indifferent owners
of the wealth of America.

Denial

The leaves are falling
ending another season
that was not hot, nor long.
The wind becomes brisker
chilling the unprepared
who did not expect
summer's quick conclusion.
Male and female machos
still wear their t-shirts
unwilling to accept
the advent of the cold,
relics of resistance
who affect nothing,
too stubborn to accept
the times are changing.

Deception

Vitriol is the fuel
that builds combustion
in the engine politic,
candidates accusing
the opposition
of every kind of crime,
confusing the voters
trying to decide
which deceiver is best
when they are unconcerned
with the needs of the nation,
the needs of the people.

Erosion of Trust

Hatred flows from the right,
fantasy spills from the left,
each violently opposed
to existence of the other,
poles so alienated
they do not allow
reasonable exchange,
leaving the great mass
of Americans
trapped in the middle
hoping for democracy,
but no longer certain
the land of the free
will nurture their children.

What Happened to Fair?

Most Americans hope
for a peaceful Election Day,
but divisions are so wide
that violence emerges
in unexpected ways,
as well as in the usual
from brutish activists
whose primary objective,
disrupt the legal process,
causes terrible harm
to the democratic system
at best a fragile contract
between humane idealists
and the overpowering rich,
determined to increase their wealth
at the expense of the people.

Achievements

Crime did not take a holiday
because it was marathon day.
Pickpockets proliferated
at pockets unregulated
by the needful protection,
looking in the wrong direction.
There was no gunfire, stabbings, fights,
in an event of delights
runners whose performance was fine,
as thousands crossed the finish line.

Unresolved Disputes

Political chaos
threatens our stability,
as claims of election theft
still permeate the land
radically dividing
the system that protects us.
The flow of information
streams 24/7
totally confusing
many Americans
who no longer know
what to believe
and cast their ballots
without conviction
that all will be well.

Disadvantaged

No matter how hard we try
to build a better life
we are often derailed
by our circumstances
that don't allow advancement,
poverty the worst burden
denying opportunity,
so many obstacles
that seemingly conspire
to prevent achievement
that lead to fulfillment.

Musings at the East River

I did not see a Cormorant
on my walk at the East River
where I once saw them daily
flying close to the surface
plunging underwater
for suicide like deep dives.
I wonder how they survive
in the polluted water
and am forced to conclude
the way of nature's existence
constant assaults by man
until so much is depleted
that it won't sustain life.

First Voyage

I try to forget
the evil I have done,
the ugliness I have seen,
not to obliterate myself,
not to exonerate myself
from what I have committed,
but in my short time remaining
to open flawed portals
to the beauty of the earth,
unexpected glimpses of the moon,
a child's smiling face,
the last chords of Beethoven,
indulgence in treasures,
renouncing guilt journeys,
savoring the pleasures
before the last horizon.

Difficult Conditions

Rain falls in the city.
Residents complain,
protest nature's assault
used to urban comfort,
so the slightest drizzle
awakens objections
to the inconvenience
of using an umbrella,
obviously forgetting
hurricanes, floods, wild fires
may not be prevented
from reaching our cities.

Stressed

The waiting room is crowded.
Everyone is urgent
to see the doctor,
then depart
before contracting
a disease
from contagious patients
dangerous to all.

Disunity

Another season goes by
and my country still endures,
though bitterly divided
over issues and values
not reconcilable
in the current climate
of extreme differences,
hatred for opponent
far more important
than banding together
to try to find answers
to the complications
disrupting the nation
in a difficult time
of increasing confusion
in the Information Age.

Twisted

Between endless images
constantly bombarding us
in the Information Age
and the manipulation
of the public's emotions
by the greedy one percent,
we turn against each other,
political positions
become far more important
than the needs of the nation,
the needs of the people.

Climbers

American politics,
a peculiar institution
that some of us consider
stranger than France, Japan,
relatively stable countries
that may not have the pathways
for the ambitious to rise
to exercise power,
except the multi-billionaires
who learn how to purchase power,
while those struggling to ascend
frequently find obstacles
preventing desired achievements,
like a former official,
a Speaker of the House,
third in succession
to the presidency,
who wanted to be president,
deprived of the position
punished the people
for his own shortcomings.

Response

Covid may be over
as a national threat,
but people are still dying.
Stress from fear of disease
still possesses many
who cannot forget
the daily death list
announced on tv
that devastated some,
was ignored by others
who were unaffected
by the pandemic.

Ire

When people do us wrong
we feel anger, rage, hate,
which leads to bitterness,
feelings of betrayal
that cloud reasoning,
prolonging inflammation
of a skewed mental state
that would be better served
reverting to calmness.

Landfall

A day in Central Park,
a new discovery
a lush garden
teeming with doves, robins,
blue jays complaining
about wary nest guards,
a flock of Canada geese
wading ashore
for us to feed them,
New Yorkers passing by
casually not noticing
our foray into nature
feeding demanding birds.

Unknown

We do not know
when we will die,
like animals
who do not know
when they will die,
unlike people
who contemplate
the condition
of life and death,
imagining
an after life
no one has seen,
while religions
make promises
of what comes next,
a wondrous place
for believers
if we have faith,
the cleansing fires
that will torment unbelievers,
both guaranteed
by the keepers
of the gates
to heaven or hell.

Hostile Attitudes

I think I know
how everything works
until I talk
to someone else
with a different view.
Then I discover
opposing beliefs
much more important
than the common good,
so someone opts to fight,
not cooperate
to solve painful problems
that affect all of us.

The Elements

The rain falls harder.
Throughout the big city
people complain
of the inconvenience
going to work, school, shop,
without understanding
where tap water comes from.
We've had less rain, less snow
even as some deny
effects of climate change.
Reservoirs must provide
water for our cities,
for rural areas,
or our toilets won't flush,
our crops will not grow.
Then we will go thirsty
before we go hungry,
a desperate problem
that rapidly becomes
a dire emergency
which could cripple our country.

Separation

There are many complaints
about what some think is wrong,
arguments, even protests
of what we object to.
With all the disputation
and deafening clamors
that the other side
did it wrong.
There never seems to be
any recognition
of the fundamental need
for us to get together
to deal with our problems,
unite for the future.

Reveries

My journey has taken me
to many people, places,
some appreciated,
too many neglected,
or used for my own needs
without sufficient return
for what they gave me.
I do not think back often,
not given to nostalgia,
but fervently hope
I have not afflicted
lasting damage
to anyone.

Relentless Grind

The poor struggle daily
to survive somehow
in a prosperous land
that has neglected them.

The working poor labor
to provide a living
for their families,
despite the resistance
of the greedy bosses
to their security.

The lower middle class
doesn't seem to realize
they are being deaccessed
by corporate rulers
who no longer need them,
except vital professions.

The middle class
may or may not persist
only by coincidence,
if fiscal stability
enables them to endure
harsh economic change.

The upper middle class
may be allowed to exist
if they have sufficient wealth

to ride out the upheavals
coming to a divided land.

To acute observers
it's painfully clear
the lords of profit
only care for the people
when they're forced to help us.

Warning Signs

The strength of diversity
is in bringing out the best
in different people
who combine to contribute
to the continuation
of a united nation.
But when we are divided
into two Americas
by political parties
hopelessly at odds
over desperate issues,
there is a terrible risk
from various enemies,
foreign and domestic,
that our country could collapse
into fractured fragments
and our once powerful land
will no longer be able
to protect our citizens.

Warm Welcome

I went to my appointment
at the doctor's office
and the place felt strange.
It took a while to notice
that everyone seemed relaxed.
The last time I was there
they were all hypertense
and exhausted looking
from tending frightened patients.
Now some of them were smiling,
a reassuring sign
the Covid threat is over.

Transient

Sooner or later
we experience
the visit of death.
If it's a loved one
it's very moving
and the loss is felt
depending how much
we loved the person..
If someone famous,
feelings are detached
from personal loss,
just the departure
of a notable
who made an impact
on the daily thread,
just not very deep
and soon forgotten.

At Risk

America the powerful
won and lost many wars
all of them abroad.
Bombs have not fallen on our land.
Foreign soldiers have not looted
our prosperous cities.
The destruction of war
has been sent to other countries.
Limited terrorist attacks
the only disturbances
of domestic tranquility,
except for shooting rampages
that threaten public order.
The extreme divisions
can lead to bitter conflict
that could fracture the nation,
delighting those who hate us
avidly waiting for collapse
that will allow many
to pillage our weakened state.
Those at home who can't agree
to get along together
are too blind to realize
they risk losing America
because they won't compromise.

We Hold…

Across this vast troubled land
divisions are splintering
the structure of unity
that once allowed us to solve
the problems that confronted us.
Unless we soon find the means
to reach accommodation
with the bitter opposition
the fabric of society
is dangerously fraying
from violent contentions
that only one side is right
and they're so adamant
they won't cooperate
for the good of the nation.

The Way

Inflation costs keep rising
forcing poor Americans
to spend more and more on food
eating up their resources,
while big corporations
make exorbitant profits
at the expense of the people
struggling to endure
as the board members
and top executives
of the voracious companies
feast on their mega yachts
without care for the rest of us
and the candidates for office
funded by the wealthy
refuse to protect us.

9/11 Remembrance

It's reassuring
on the anniversary
of a day of infamy,
terrorist attack
that took so many lives
of unwary innocents
that so many remember
in a troubled land
that quickly forgets
the unpalatable.
Our hope for the future
is that concerned agencies
will better monitor
our many enemies
who bitterly hate us,
in order to protect us
from those who wish us harm.

Sniveling Losers

The pace of vehemence
mostly ugly rhetoric
accelerates daily
as we approach election day,
once a celebration
of our democracy,
once the envy of the world.
Now many candidates
deny legitimacy
of the 2020 election,
creating a precedent
to deny the results
if they lose this election.

www.ingramcontent.com/pod-product-compliance
Ingram Content Group UK Ltd.
Pitfield, Milton Keynes, MK11 3LW, UK
UKHW021341190726
13845UKWH00027B/656

9 789363 546202